The Wheels on the Bus

go round and round

Kate Toms

make
believe
ideas

The **wheels** on the bus go
round and round, all day long!

go round and round

The driver on the bus says,
All aboard,
all aboard,
all aboard.

Ticket 1. 2. 3

32town
BUS 1

The driver on the bus says,
All aboard,
all day long!

go round and round

The babies on the bus go
wah, wah, wah,
wah, wah, wah,
wah, wah, wah!

The babies on the bus go
wah, wah, wah,

all day long!

go round and round

The grandads on the bus say,
What's that noise?
What's that noise?
What's that noise?
The grandads on the bus say,
What's that noise?
all day long!

go round and round

The horn on the bus goes

beep, beep, beep,

beep, beep, beep,

beep, beep, beep.

The horn on the bus goes

beep, beep, beep,

all day long!

go round and round

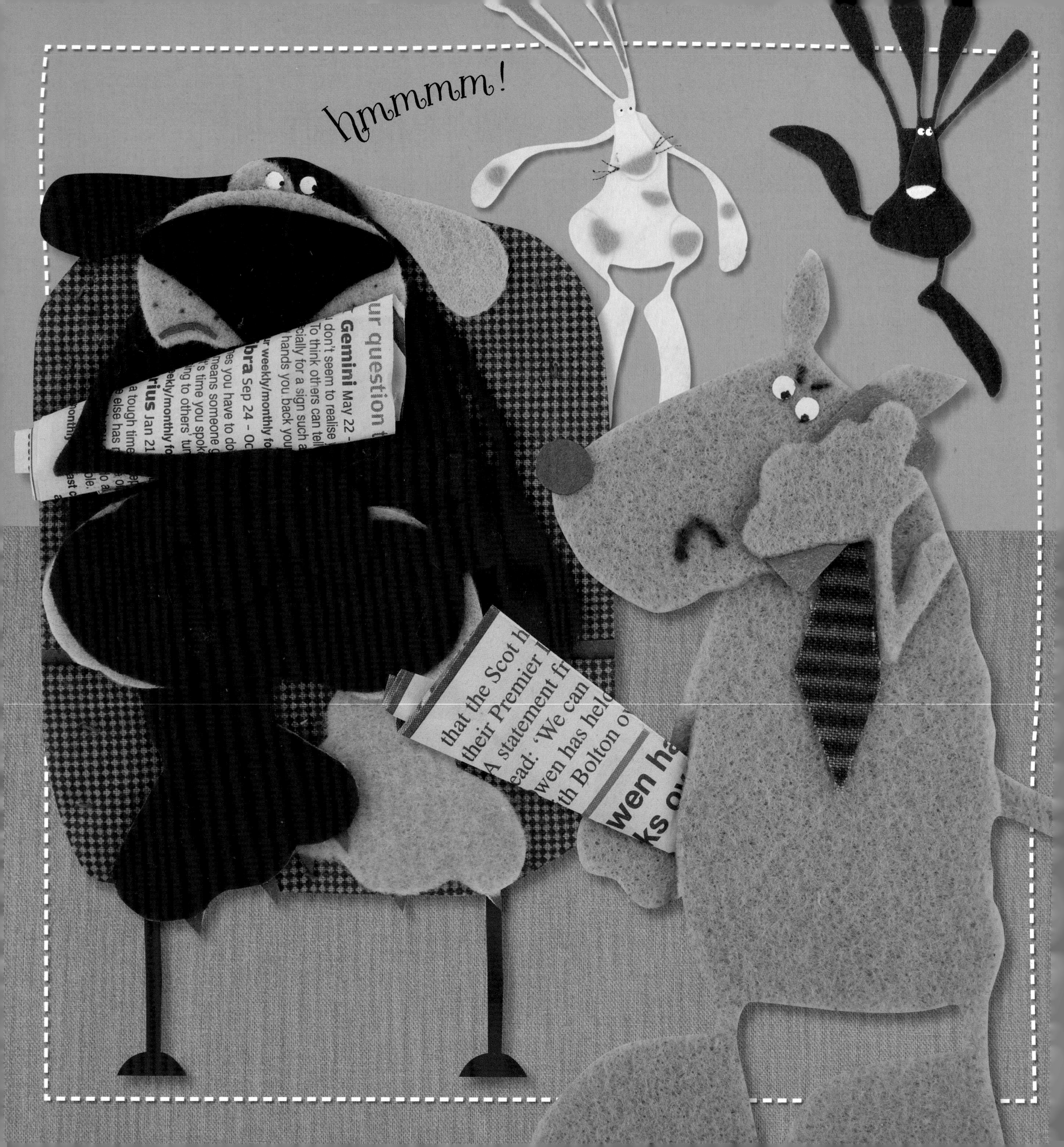
hmmmm!

The **boys** on the bus just horse around, horse around, horse around.

The **boys** on the bus just horse around, all day long!

Can you do this?

The **nannies** on the bus go
Knit, Knit, Knit,
Knit, Knit, Knit,
Knit, Knit, Knit.
The **nannies** on the bus go
Knit, Knit, Knit,
all day long!

go round and round

Nice scarf, Doris

The **wheels** on the bus go round and round,
round and round,
round and round.
The **wheels** on the bus go
round and round,
bye-bye!
all day long!